Cindy Lurie
Blessed
Mary Angela

This book is lovingly dedicated to all at St. Francis Residence, and the Felician Sisters, Franciscan Friars and Brothers at Our Lady of the Angels Convent in Enfield, CT.

Blessed Mary Angela

Written by
Cindy Lurie

Illustrated by
Aaron Nethaneel

Blessed Mary Angela,
We seek your loving way.
Help us to be grateful
For the newness of each day.

St. Francis and St. Felix,
And dear St. Joseph, too
Opened up your loving heart
To pray, and give, and do.

So, to the poor and orphaned;
The homeless, and the ill
You gave unending service
Following God's Will.

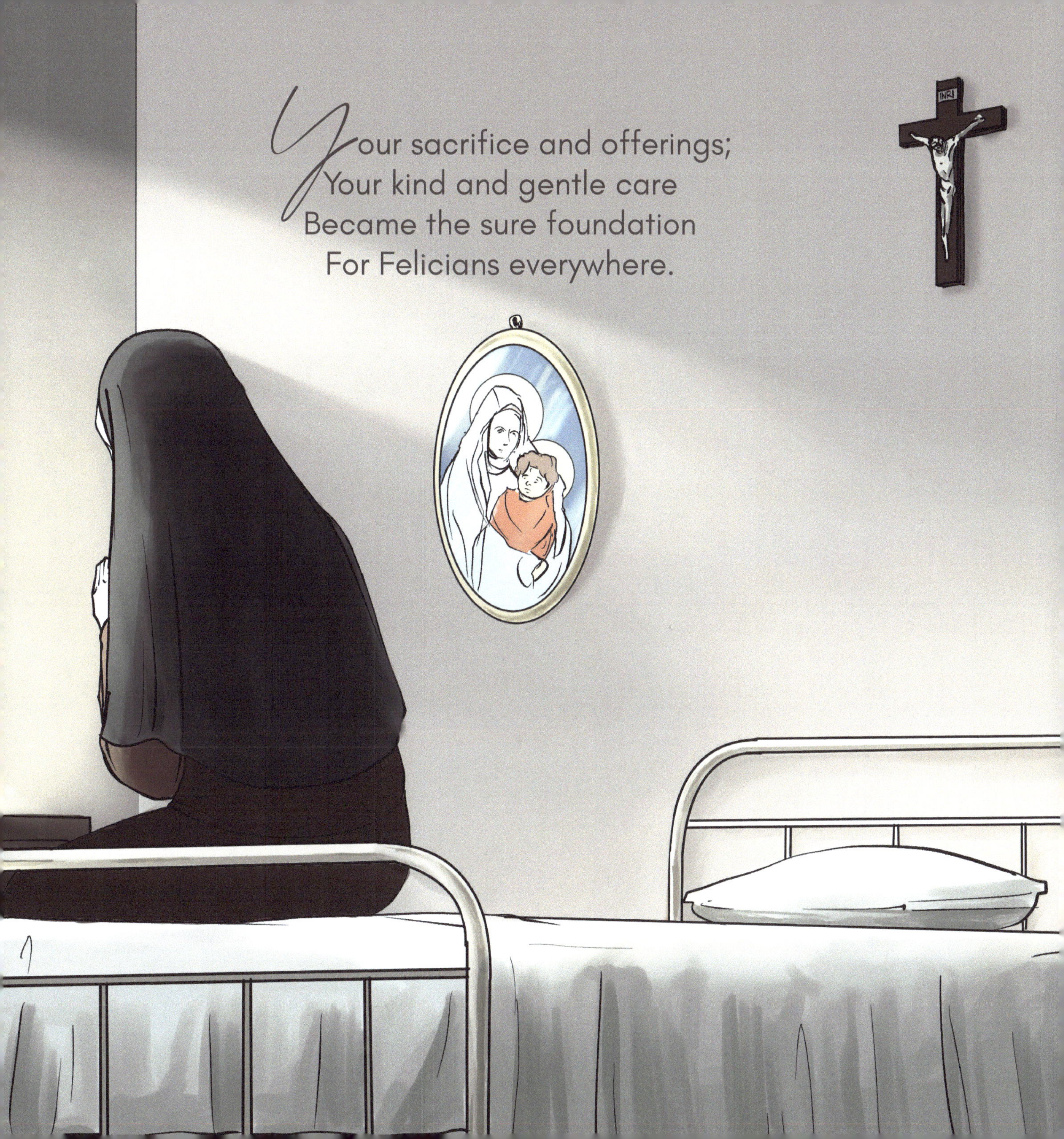

Your sacrifice and offerings;
Your kind and gentle care
Became the sure foundation
For Felicians everywhere.

As Foundress of this order,
With Mary by your side,
Felician Sisters flourished
Throughout the whole world wide!

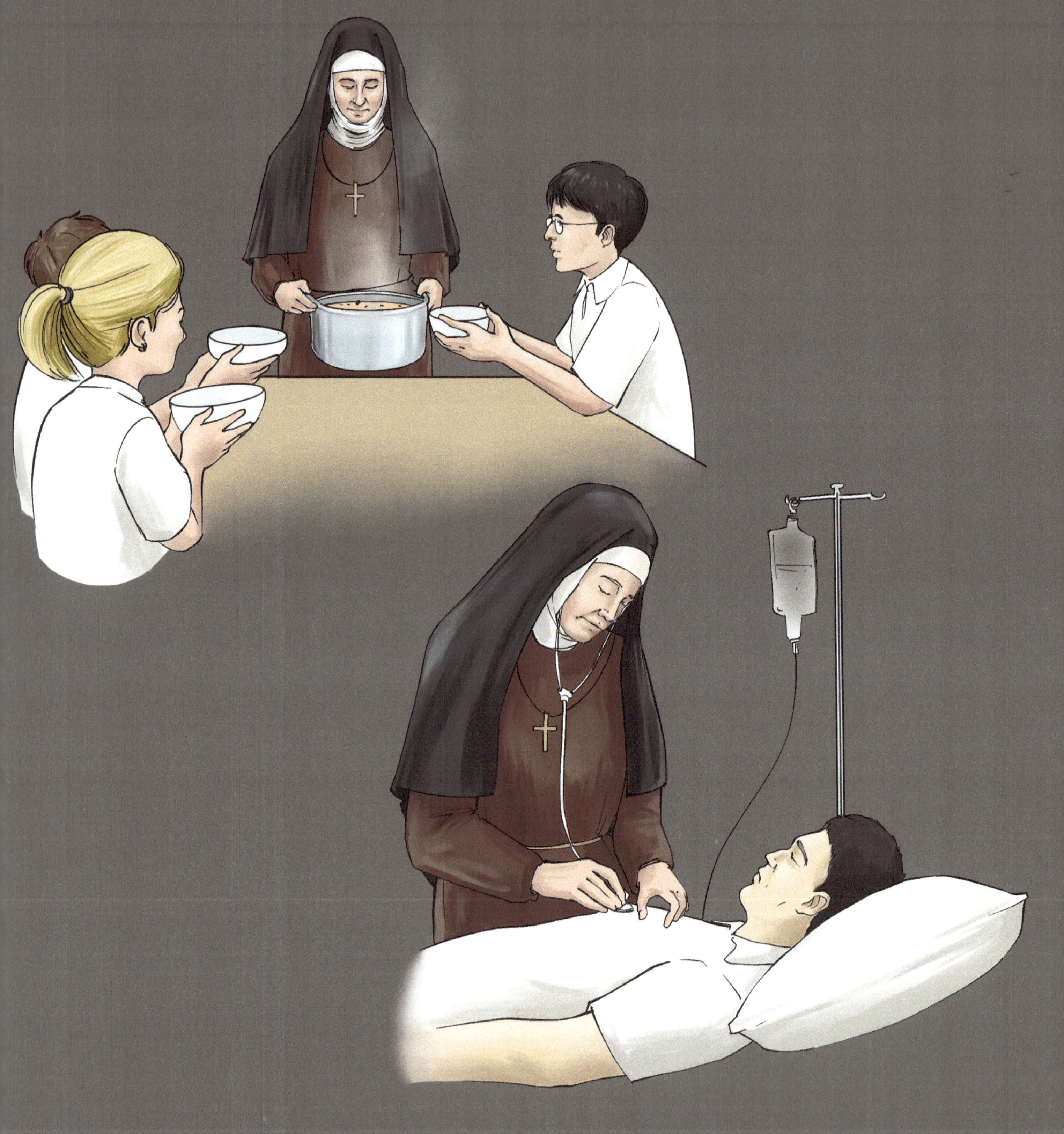

As blessed, holy women,
In clinic, mission, school,
They follow very lovingly
The dear Franciscan Rule.

Oh Blessed Mary Angela,
We pray a saint you'll be.
For you have given hope and love,
And set the lonely free.

Along with Jesus, you have taught
That service, faith, and trust
Will bring about a world of peace
Where all are true and just.

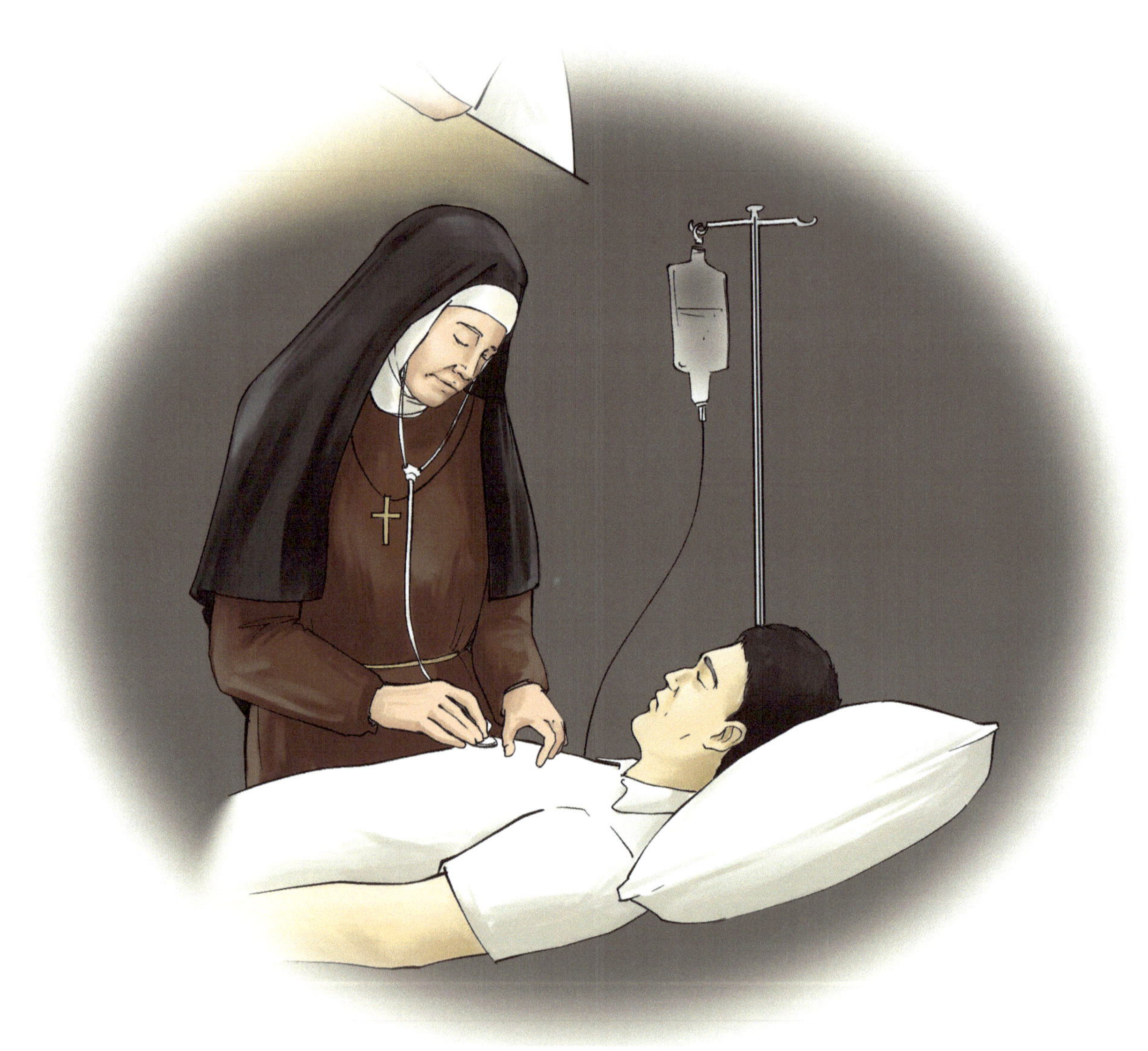